The Little Avant-Garde

A Piano Method for Pre-Schoolers
by S T E P H E N   C O V E L L O

THIRD REVISED EDITION

ISBN 0-7935-3981-1

G. SCHIRMER, Inc.

DISTRIBUTED BY

HAL•LEONARD®
CORPORATION

7777 W. BLUEMOUND RD. P.O. BOX 13819 MILWAUKEE, WI 53213

TABLE OF CONTENTS

PREFACE

THE LITTLE AVANT-GARDE is an innovative piano method based on preschoolers' unsupervised improvisations at the piano. As a collection of expressive piano solos using easy-to-read notation, teachers will discover that THE LITTLE AVANT-GARDE is a most pleasurable, imaginative, and easy way to prepare the very young student for primer level piano.

THE LITTLE AVANT-GARDE intends to:
1. Give students a rich musical experience at the piano using physical movements akin to their natural vocabulary of movement.
2. Present lesson pages in large, clear, uncluttered notation.
3. Put the entire keyboard at their disposal from the first lesson.
4. Give students the pleasure of creating their own music through improvisation.
5. Involve students with the elements of interpretation from the outset.
6. Present music of such nature as to enable students to express a wide range of emotions.
7. Present elements of both traditional and contemporary music.

The goals at the top of each lesson page were written to be understood, as often as possible, by the student and may be read aloud by the teacher. The unnumbered comments which follow are directed to the teacher.

In closing, the author wishes to acknowledge Susie Covello's contributions toward the text, imaginative titles for many of the pieces, and critical comments about the music and the final shape and format of THE LITTLE AVANT-GARDE.

Stephen Covello

Central Nyack, New York

PART I

KEY TO MUSICAL SYMBOLS EMPLOYED
IN THE LITTLE AVANT-GARDE
(Numbers to the left refer to examples shown in ILLUSTRATION ONE)

Line A shows musical symbols employed in THE LITTLE AVANT-GARDE. Line B shows one of the many possible interpretations of these symbols, written in standard notation.

1. The horizontal line bisecting the system of notation represents Middle C.
2. "Above Middle C" means those keys located to the right of Middle C.
3. "Below Middle C" means those keys located to the left of Middle C.
4. A black ellipse above or below Middle C is a single improvised note held for a short time (a pulse or beat) on a white key.
5. A black ellipse followed by numbers under a bracket represents a single, improvised note on a white key held for the count indicated.
6. A dashed line diagonally connecting two notes from left to right indicates that the second note is played as soon as the first is completed.
7. A black note on the Middle C line is Middle C.
8. A black note shaped like a tulip is a tone cluster improvised on the white keys and held for a short time.
9. A black note shaped like a tulip followed by numbers under a bracket is an improvised tone cluster on the white keys held for the count indicated.
10. Two pairs of vertical dashed lines separated by numbers indicates a rest for both hands for the counts shown.
11. A rectangle indicates that the notes within are played with both hands together.
12. A bracketed number above several notes indicates the quantity of notes in that series.
13. The further above the Middle C line a note is written, the higher the note; the further below the Middle C line a note is written, the lower the note.
14. A rectangle with numbers under a bracket extending from the upper right corner indicates that all notes in the rectangle are held for the count indicated.
15. Two note series in a rectangle indicates that notes in both series are played simultaneously.

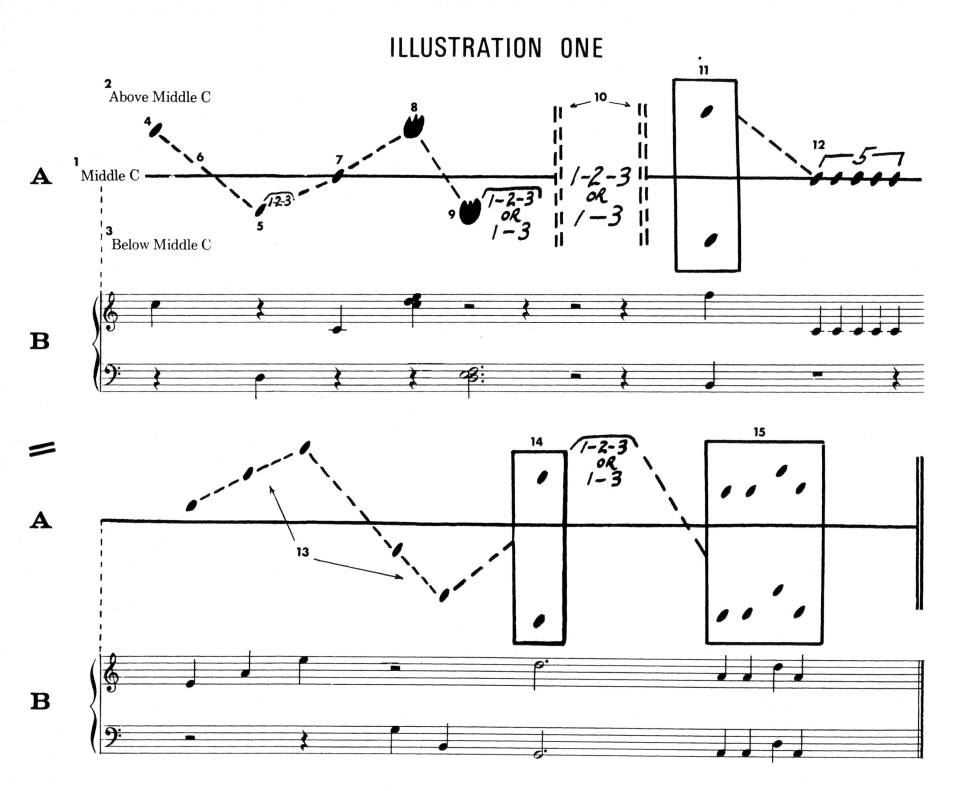

LESSON 1

1. Learn to find MIDDLE C on the PIANO KEYBOARD.
2. See the LONG LINE for middle C on the lesson page.
3. Show which KEYS are above middle C and show which NOTES are above the middle C line; show which are below.
4. See the sign and learn to play SHORT BLACK NOTES on WHITE KEYS.
5. Read from left to right and lift finger when each note is finished.
6. The DASHED LINE tells you to play the second note as soon as the first note ends.
7. See the DOUBLE BAR, showing the end of the piece.

All single notes are played with the index finger. All notes above middle C are played with the right hand. All notes below middle C are played with the left hand.

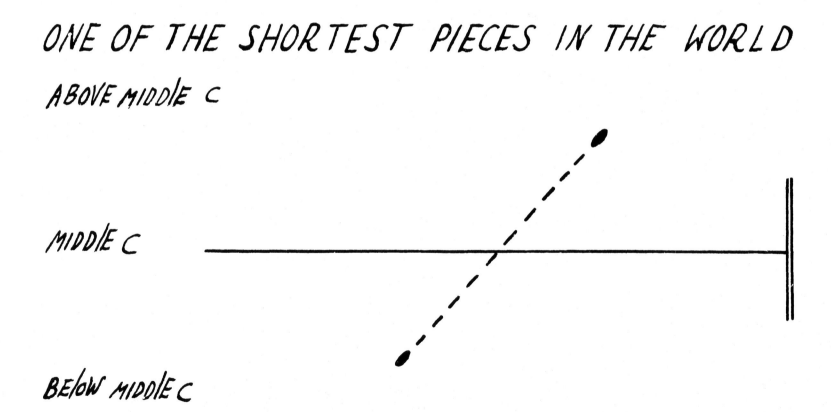

ONE OF THE SHORTEST PIECES IN THE WORLD

ABOVE MIDDLE C

MIDDLE C

BELOW MIDDLE C

LESSON 2

1. Learn to play COUNT NOTES.
2. Learn to play and count out loud slowly and evenly.

Counting begins as the note is struck. All playing is moderately slow unless a tempo marking indicates otherwise.

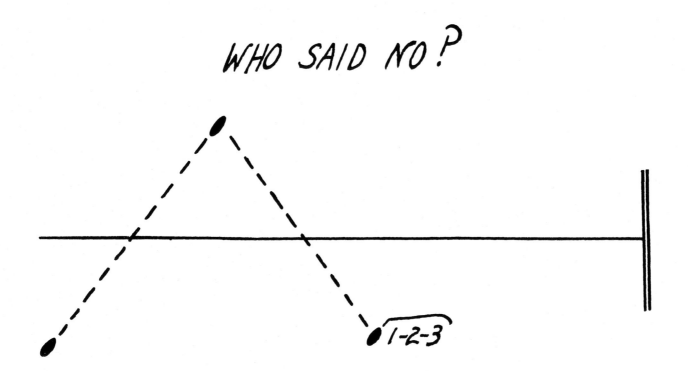

LESSON 3

1. Begin the habit of looking ahead while playing count notes to get ready for the next note.
2. Learn to change from high and low notes to MIDDLE C with the same hand.

When middle C is played in a sequence, using alternate hands is preferred. If middle C is preceded by a rest, either hand may be used.

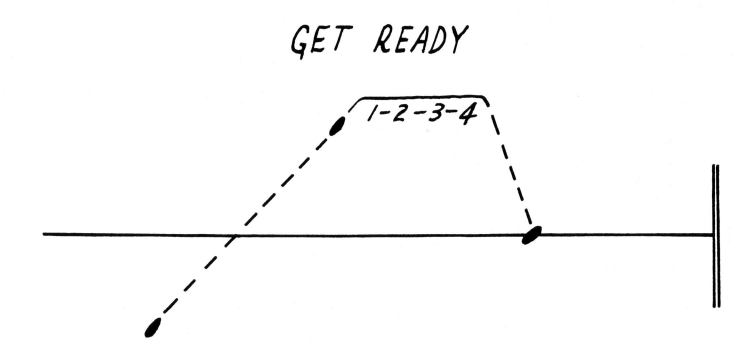

LESSON 4

1. See the sign and learn to pick finger up at the beginning of a rest.
2. Begin to play SHORT BLACK NOTES the same speed as "COUNT" NOTES and RESTS.
3. Begin the habit of looking ahead during rests to get ready for the next note.

LEFT RIGHT, LEFT RIGHT

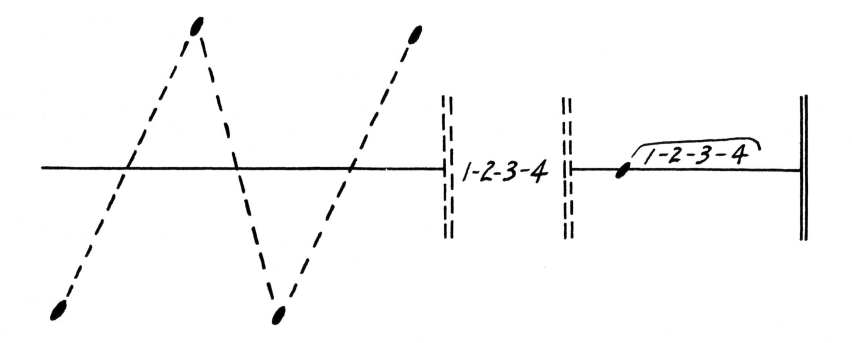

LESSON 5

1. See the sign and learn to play short TULIP NOTES.
2. Learn to play different kinds of notes in the same piece.

"Tulip notes" are played by making a fist and striking several white keys at once with the area between the first and second joints of the fingers.

KNUCKLE DOWN

LESSON 6

1. See the sign and learn to play BOTH HANDS TOGETHER.

The tone clusters in the rectangle should be played precisely together.

CRUNCH !

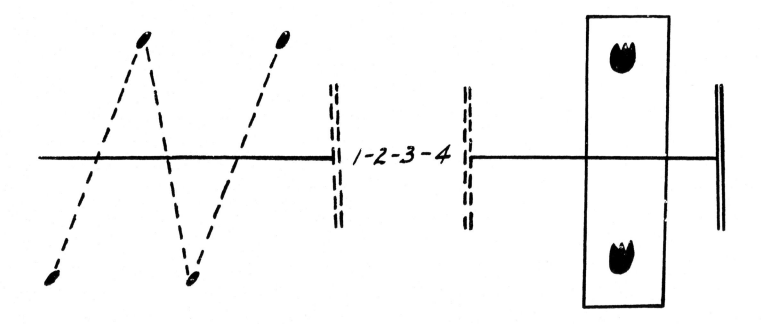

1-2-3-4

LESSON 7

1. Learn to play different count notes in the same piece.
2. Keep playing and counting evenly.

SHORTER AND SHORTER

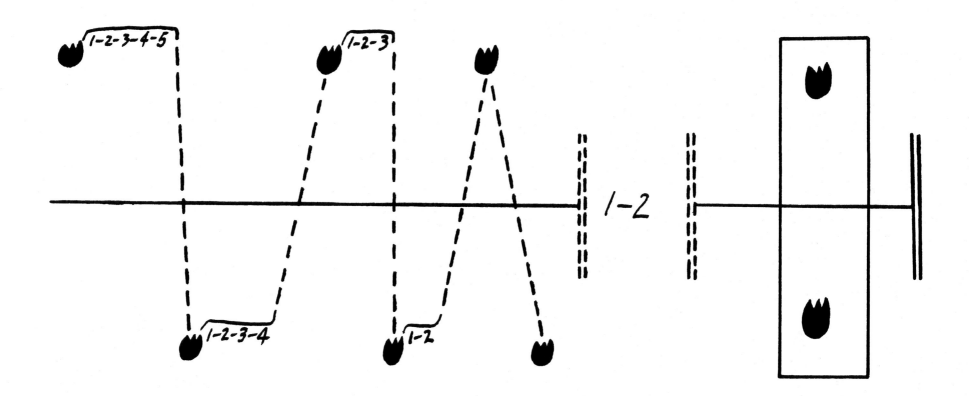

LESSON 8

1. Learn to change from one kind of note to another with no rest in between.

THE FIRST TIME I PLAYED THE PIANO

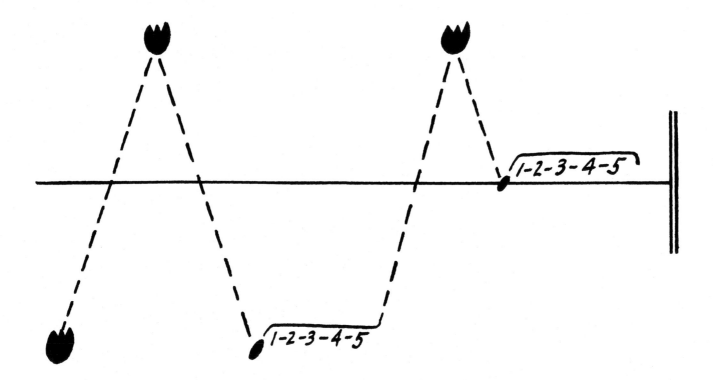

LESSON 9

1. See the name of Lesson 9, EXERCISES, meaning bits of music to be played many times to help get strong fingers.
2. See the sign and learn to play and count five notes evenly on the same key. We call these NOTE SERIES.
3. See the signs and learn to play LOUD or SOFT.
4. See the signs and learn to play LOUDER or SOFTER, LITTLE BY LITTLE.
5. See and learn to use the REPEAT SIGN.

   The student should always count 1-2-3-4-5 aloud when playing five-note series.

EXERCISES

LESSON 10

1. Find loud and soft signs in a piece.
2. Learn to play loud or soft notes at the right time, evenly.

GEORGIE, GEORGIE

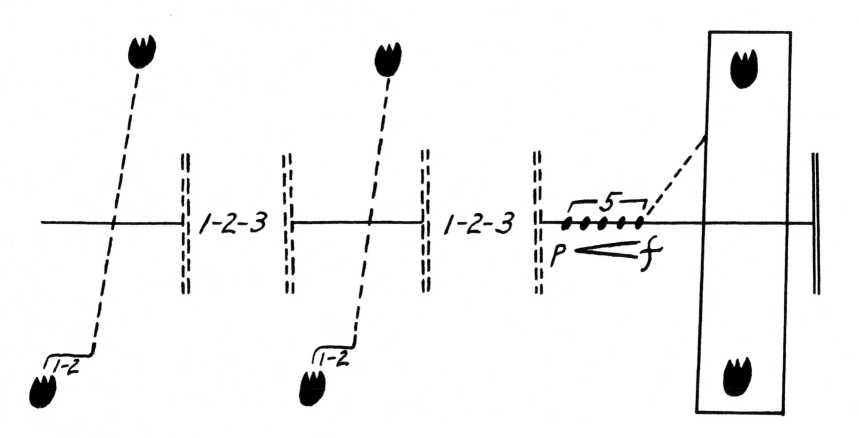

LESSON 11

1. See the signs and learn to play ACCENTED NOTES.

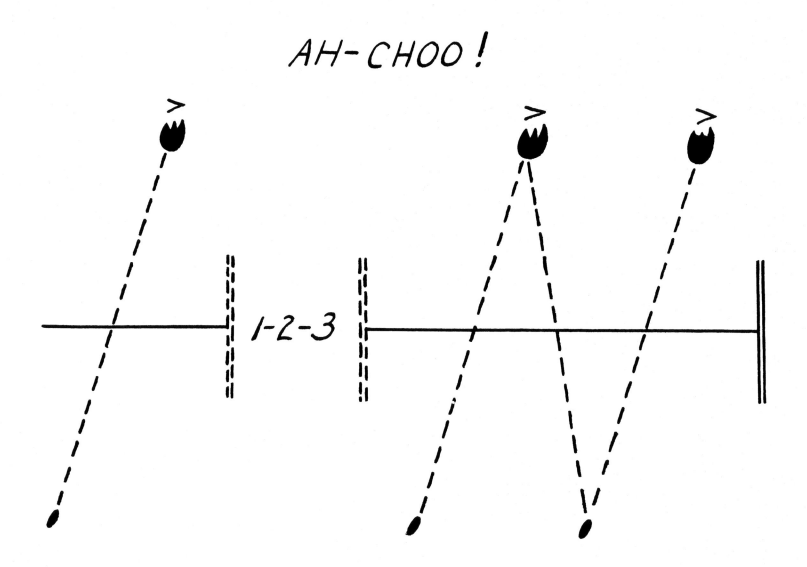

LESSON 12

1. Learn to play a two-line piece, always reading from left to right.
2. Learn to play a long piece smoothly and evenly, especially when going from the first to the second line.
3. See the sign and learn to play "COUNT" NOTES, BOTH HANDS TOGETHER.

MAKING FRIENDS WITH A BIG DOG

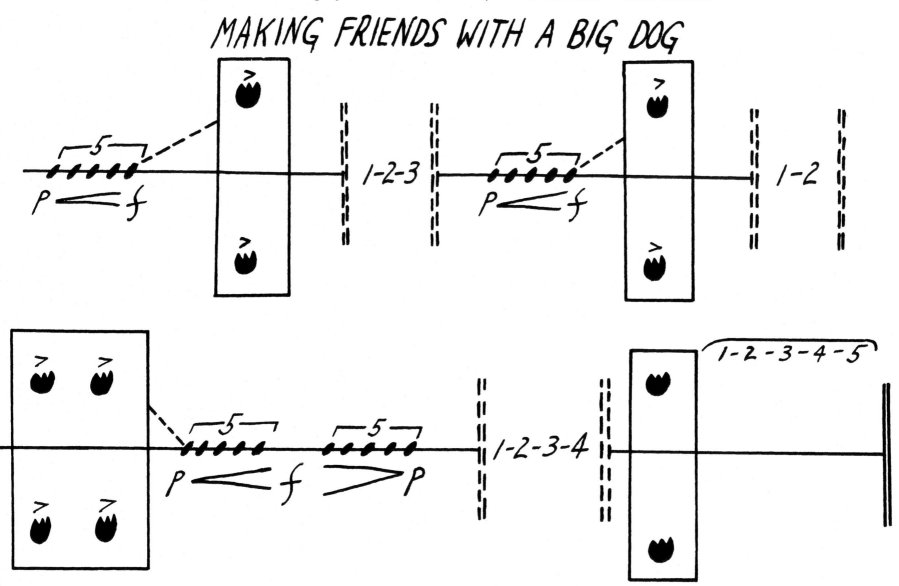

LESSON 13

1. See the sign and learn to play the STACCATO or "bounce" note.
2. See the word and learn the meaning of the TEMPO mark ALLEGRO. Tempo means how fast or slow to play.
3. See and learn to use the FERMATA sign as a pause.
4. See the signs and learn to play VERY LOUD or VERY SOFT.

THE PIECE ON THE COVER

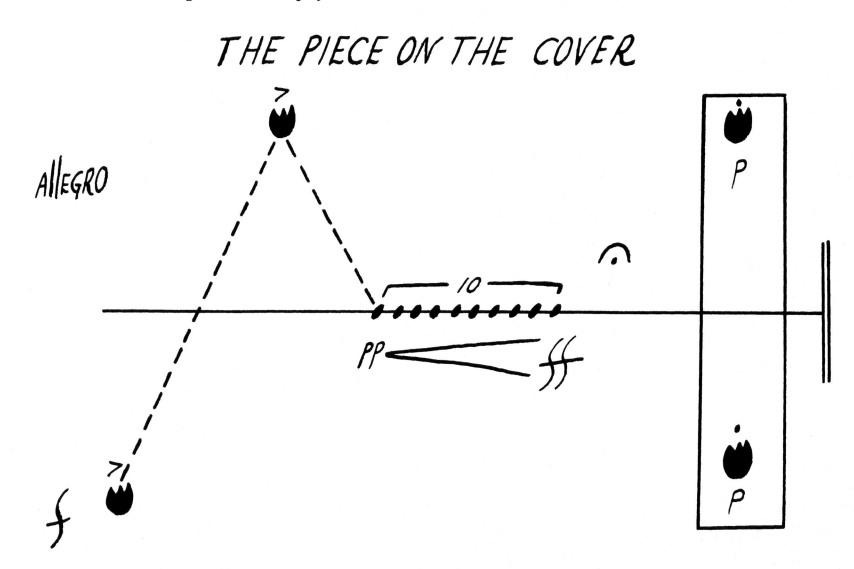

1. See the R. H., telling the right hand to play, and L. H., telling the left hand to play.
2. The right hand learns to play higher and higher notes by LEAPING to the right, away from middle C.
3. See how the pictures of higher notes go up toward the top of the page.
4. The left hand learns to play lower and lower notes by leaping to the left, away from middle C.
5. See how pictures of lower notes go down toward the bottom of the page.
6. Learn to move hands quickly from one spot to another on the piano keyboard.

Leaps in each hand should be less than an octave so that the highest and lowest notes of the piece are well within the student's reach. The ten-note series is played all on the same key.

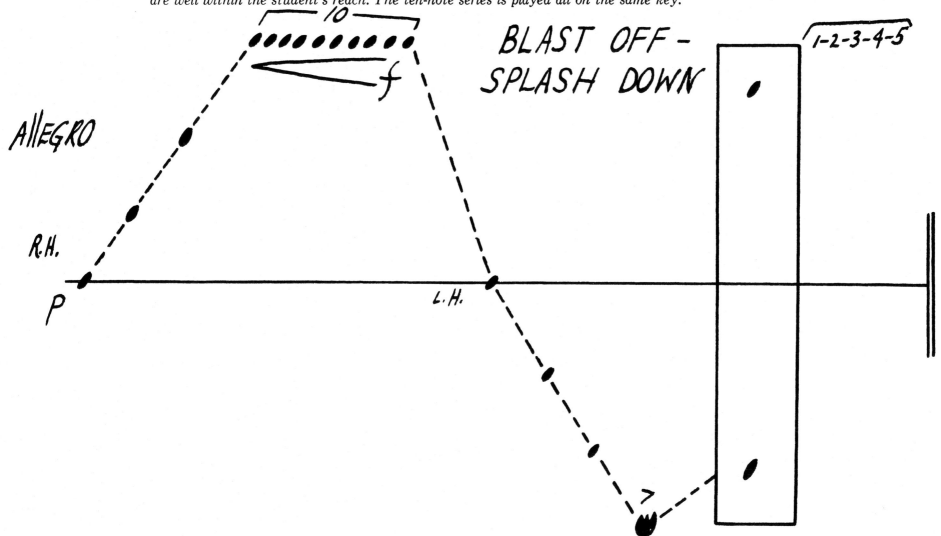

LESSON 15

1. See that when music is turned upside down, the beginning becomes the end, the end becomes the beginning, the high notes become the low notes and the low notes become the high notes.

To play UPSIDE DOWN CAKE PART II, turn book upside down and play piece as it then appears. The student may choose his or her own tempo and dynamics.

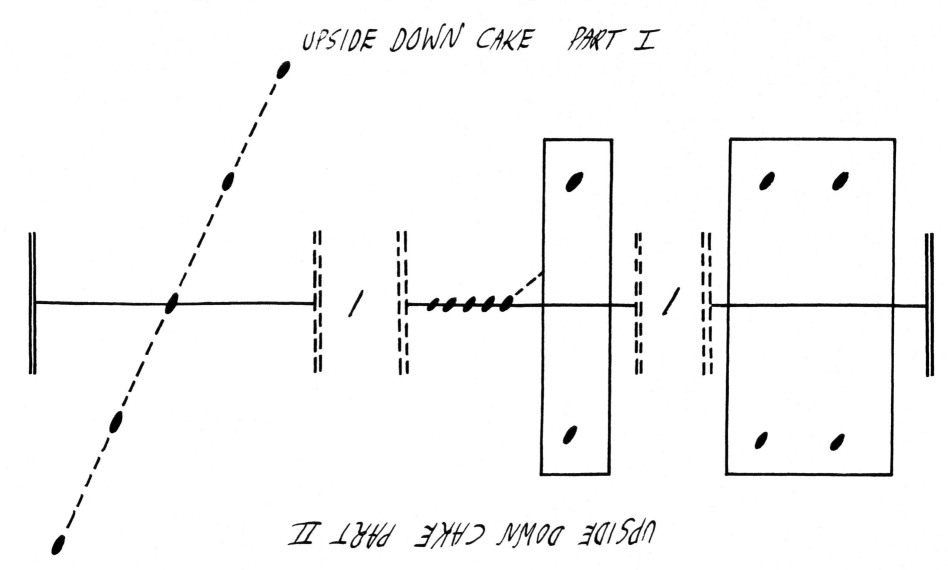

UPSIDE DOWN CAKE   PART I

ᴜᴘꜱɪᴅᴇ ᴅᴏᴡɴ ᴄᴀᴋᴇ ᴘᴀʀᴛ ɪɪ

1. See the word and learn the meaning of the tempo mark ANDANTE.
2. See the sign and learn to play TENUTO.
3. Learn to play and count five notes evenly on the same keys, hands together.

IN AND OUT THE DOOR

LESSON 17

1. Learn to leap back and forth with the right hand over the left hand and middle C.
2. See the numbers 1-4 under the bracket, telling you to count 1-2-3-4.

OVER THE C

ANDANTE

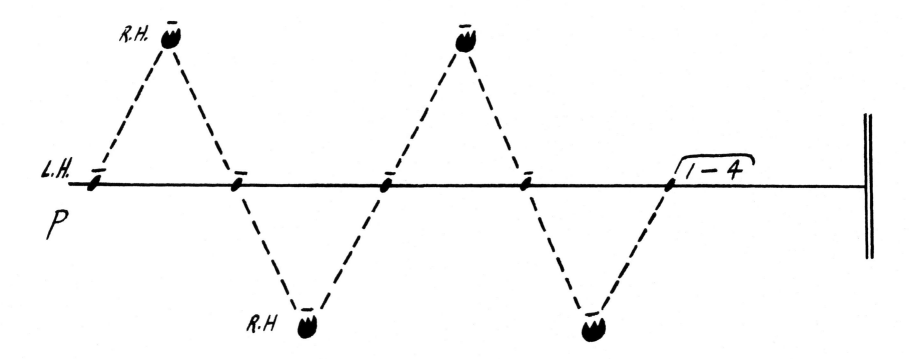

1. See the word STACCATO.
2. Learn to play and count a five-note series of staccato notes slowly and evenly on the same key.

   The student should think of staccato as motion away from the key.

SALT AND PEPPER

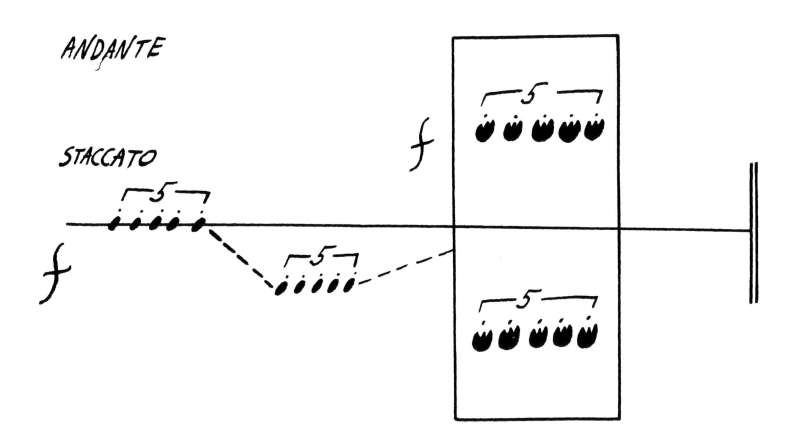

LESSON 19

1. Learn to play two kinds of notes at the same time.

PICKING UP MY TOYS

ANDANTE

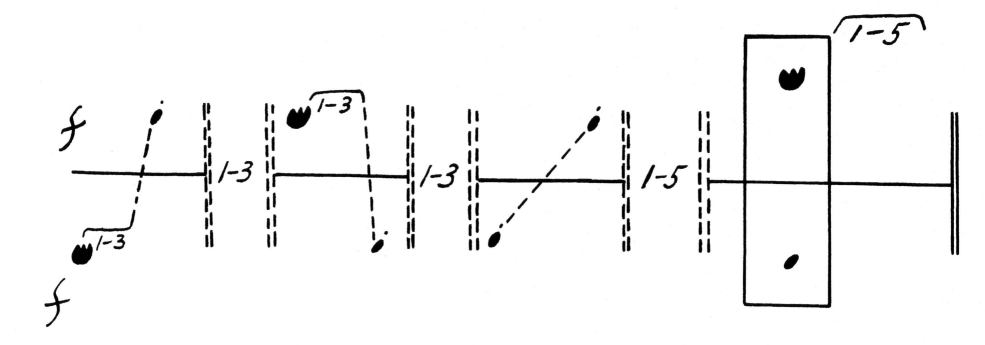

1. Learn to play and count leaping notes evenly in a series.
2. In line 2, see that the right-hand note series go higher and the left-hand note series go lower.
3. In line 2, see that the tempo marking changes from Allegro to Andante.
4. See and learn to use the FERMATA sign as a hold.

JUMPING BEAN

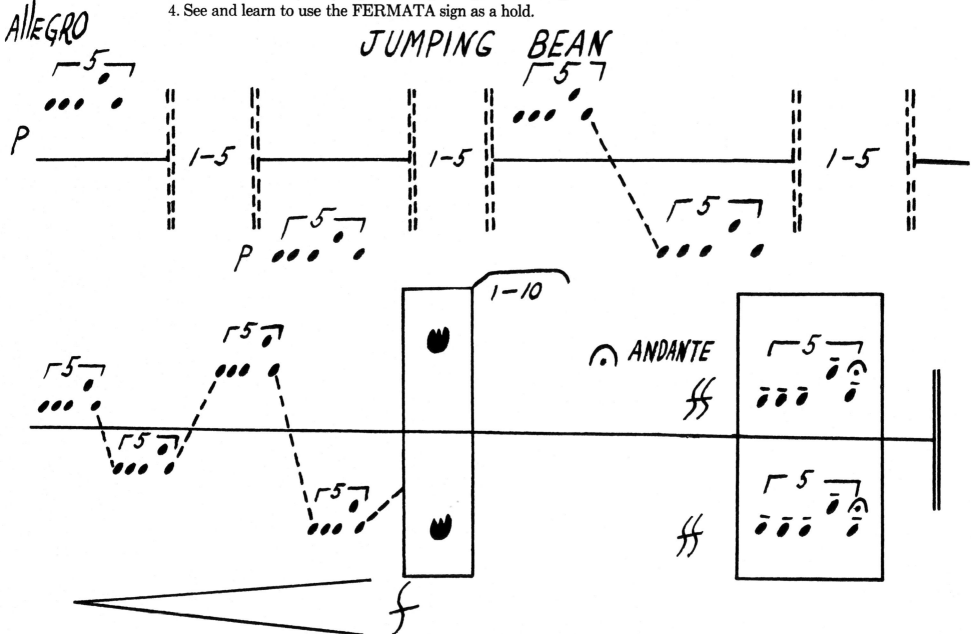

PART II

KEY TO MUSICAL SYMBOLS EMPLOYED IN
THE LITTLE AVANT-GARDE, PART II
(Numbers to the left refer to examples shown in ILLUSTATION TWO)

Line A shows musical symbols employed in **THE LITTLE AVANT-GARDE**. Line B shows one
of the many possible interpretations of those symbols, written in standard notation.

1. A note on a line is a line note and a note just above or just below a line is a space note. Notes moving in one direction from a space to a line or a line to a space represent stepwise motion from one white key to another.
2. A sharp sign just before Middle C is C♯.
3. A natural sign cancels a previously applied accidental.
4. An improvised white-key note followed by a sharped note on the same level means the second note is a half step higher than the first note. The white key chosen must be a half step below a black key.
5. A black ellipse with a sharp represents a single, improvised note held for a short time on a black key.
6. A black note shaped like a tulip with a sharp is a tone cluster played on the black keys and is held for a short time.

ILLUSTRATION TWO

LESSON 21

1. Learn to name fingers by numbers.

The student opens the book on his or her lap, or on a table, and places his or her hands on the pictured outlines. Starting with the right thumb, he or she taps one finger at a time and identifies its number; the left the same. The teacher may spend a short time playing the game of calling numbers at random for the child to tap.

FINGER GAME

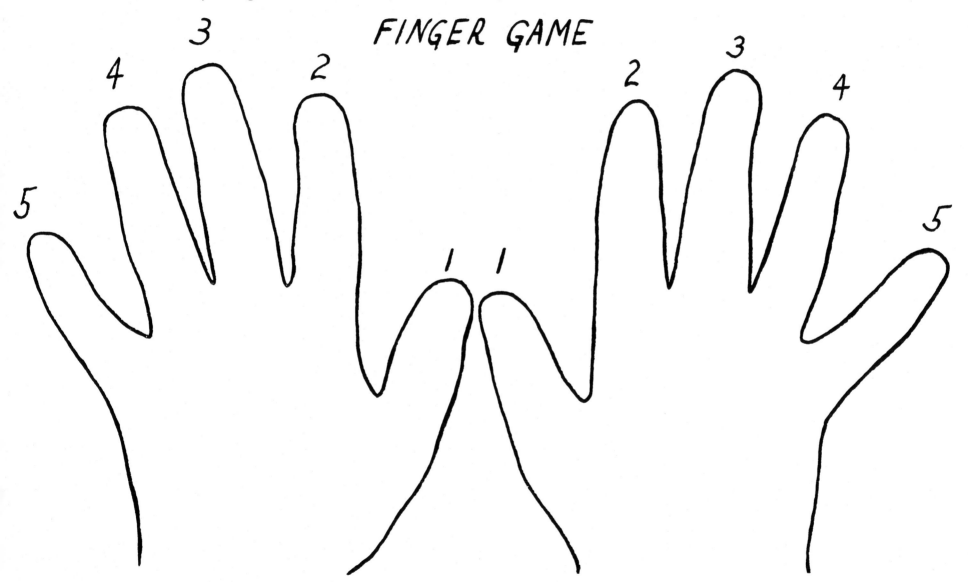

LESSON 22

1. See notes on lines followed by notes in spaces, telling that the second note is the next white key. This is one way of playing by steps.

EXERCISE IN STEPWISE MOTION

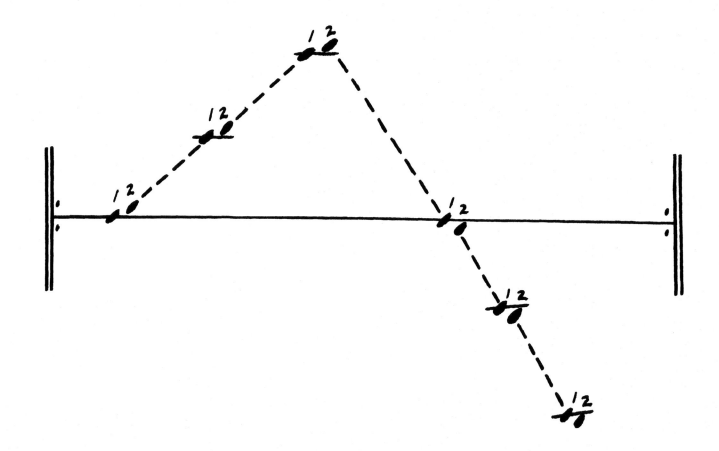

LESSON 23

1. See three notes going up or down by step.
2. Learn to play three notes going by step using fingers 1, 2, and 3.
3. See the SLUR sign and learn to play LEGATO.

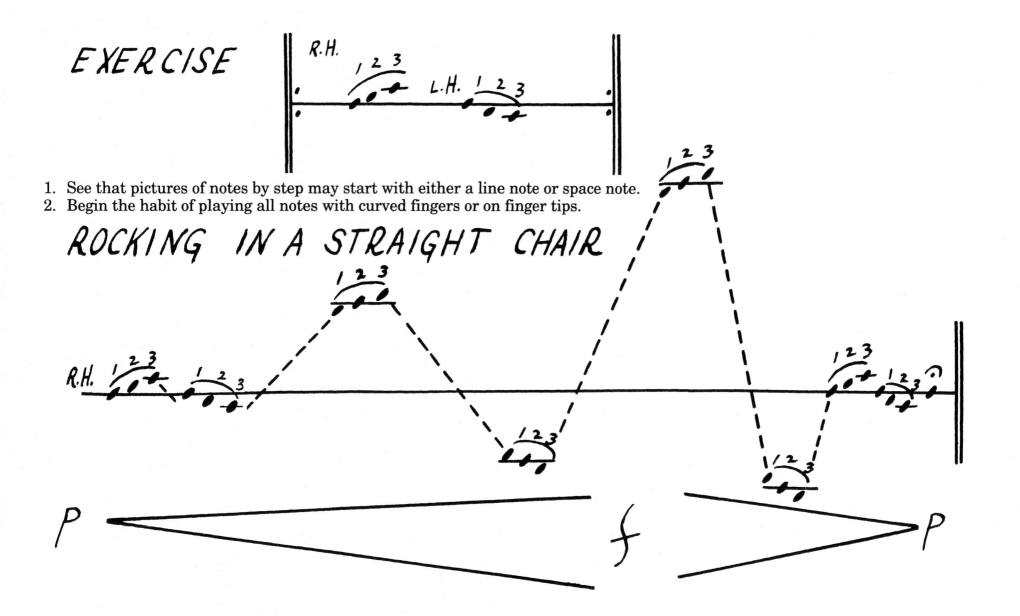

1. See that pictures of notes by step may start with either a line note or space note.
2. Begin the habit of playing all notes with curved fingers or on finger tips.

ROCKING IN A STRAIGHT CHAIR

LESSON 24

1. Learn to play by step with both hands together.
2. See the sign and learn to play MEDIUM LOUD.

WAVES IN A PUDDLE

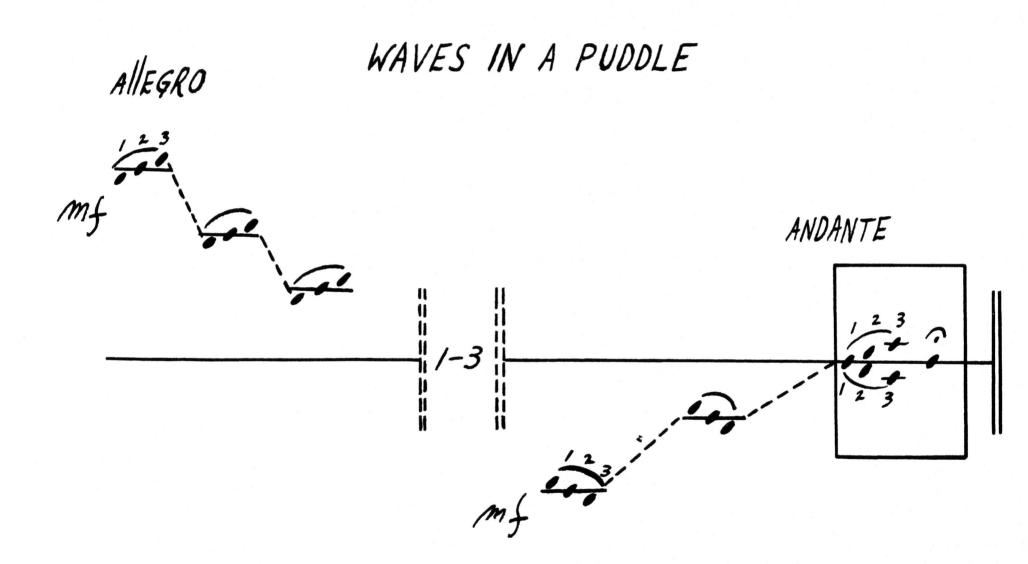

LESSON 25

1. See the sign and learn to play the C SHARP on a BLACK KEY.

THE PIECE WITH THE EXTRA NOTE

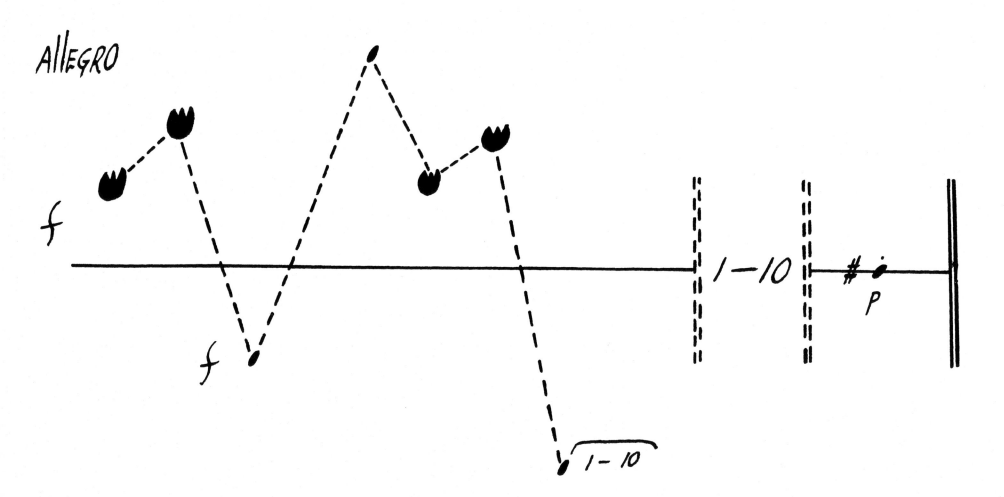

LESSON 26

1. See the word and learn the meaning of the tempo mark MODERATO.
2. See black notes followed by sharped black notes, telling that the second note is the next black key to the right of the first one played.
3. Choose white keys carefully in this piece. Look for one with a black key to the right of it.

THE STORY OF 2 FALLING LEAVES

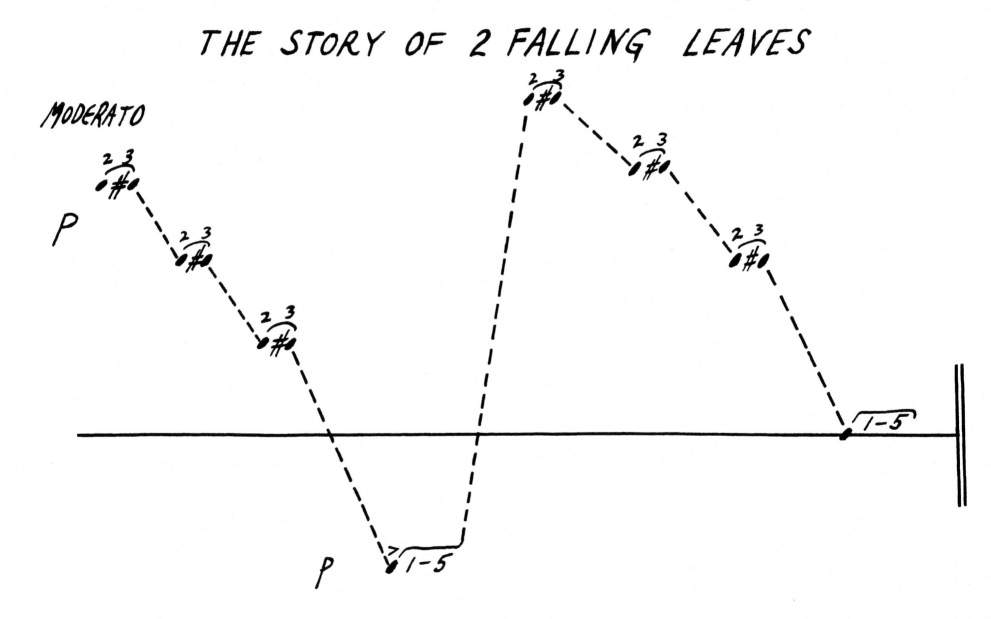

1. See the sign and learn to play tulip notes on black keys.

CHOO CHOO

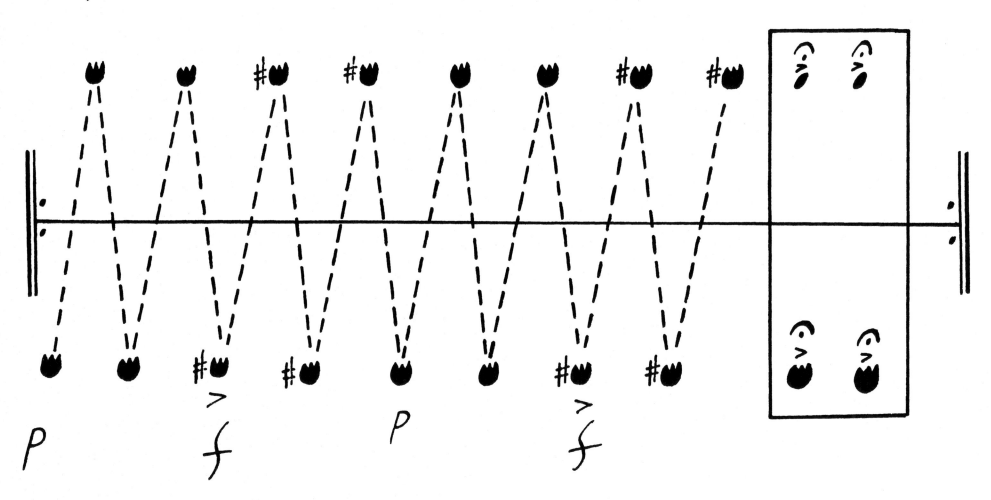

LESSON 28

1. See the sign and learn to play the NATURAL.
2. Learn to leap without moving hand by playing finger 3, then finger 1.

EXERCISES

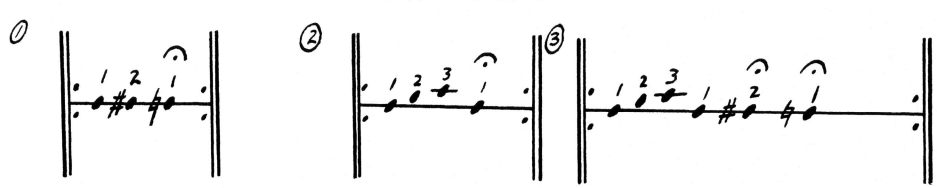

1. Learn to play both sharps and naturals in a piece.

THIS WAY, THAT WAY

ANDANTE

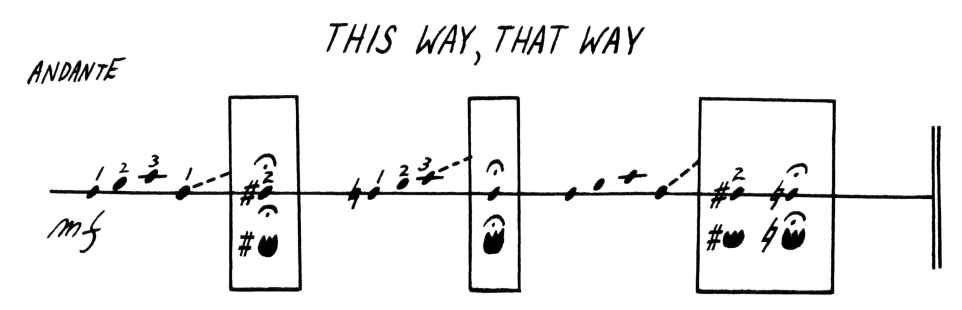

LESSON 29

1. See the sign and learn to play tulip notes on black keys.

The student should start playing far enough away from middle C so he or she can perform the piece as written.

SQUEE JAW

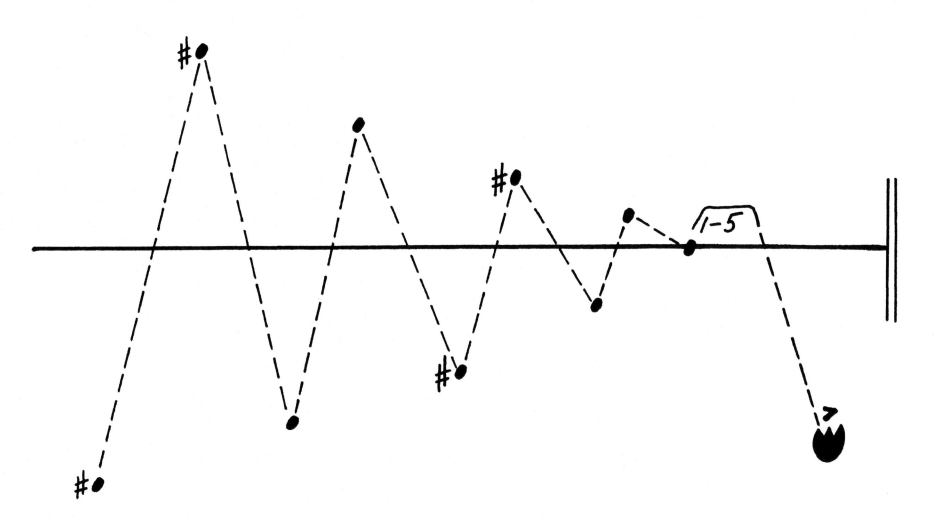

1. Remember how to play by steps.
2. See that 1, 2, 3 fingering will be used on all note series in this piece, even when not written in.

STAR PICTURES

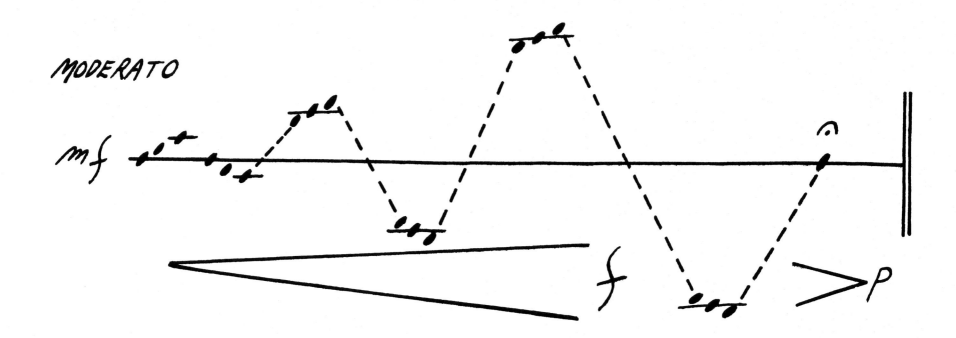